When you responded to God's love by inviting Jesus Christ into your life, you began an exciting journey that will lead you into a wonderful new life with God and His family.

Welcome to the journey and welcome to the family!

A small seed contains life with tremendous potential. If placed in the right soil and given the right care, it will become a large plant and produce wonderful fruit. Between the seed and its fruit, however, there will be stages of growth.

What is true in the natural world is true in the spiritual world also. As a new Christian, you have begun a life that must be nurtured to maturity.

You're off to a good start. Let's keep it going! Here is what you can do to grow strong and healthy as a believer in Jesus Christ.

A *Story* with *You* in *Mind*

Jesus told a story about a farmer who scattered seed in anticipation of a great harvest. The point of the story was that seeds need good soil in order to grow.

In the story, some of the farmer's seed fell along a path where the ground had been packed hard by foot traffic. Because the ground was hard and the seed could not take root quickly, birds ate it.

Other seed fell among rocks and shallow soil. The seed quickly sprouted, but because there was no depth to the soil, the seedlings dried up and died when the sun came out.

Still other seed fell to the ground among weeds. It sprouted, but the weeds competed with the new plants and choked them out.

Some seed, however, fell on good soil where it took root, grew strong, and produced a great crop.

Jesus told this story with you in mind. You can read it in the thirteenth chapter of the book of Matthew in the Bible.

God's seed has been scattered upon the soil of your life in anticipation of good things. That seed took root when you received Jesus Christ as your Savior. God wants to nurture that new life in you so that you will grow strong and bear fruit. If that is to happen, you must continue to provide good soil—a receptive heart—in which God can develop this new and exciting life.

As you begin your life as a Christian, what good changes do you expect?

Unlike the path, packed hard by foot traffic, your heart was soft enough for God's seed to take root. What made you open to God's work in your life?

Take a minute to thank God for the new life that has taken root in you.

God has Planted His Seed in You

God was at work around the edges of your life even before you knew He cared. He has always been present in the situations and events of your life, waiting for you to allow Him to plant a new life within you. That's called *grace*.

The Bible says, "For it is by grace you have been saved, through faith—and this not from yourselves, it is the gift of God—not by works, so that no one can boast" (Ephesians 2:8–9).

When you accepted Christ as your Savior, God forgave all of your past sins. He adopted you into His family. He gave you His Spirit to strengthen and guide you. He gave you an eternal life. These are things only He can do. They are His gift to you.

God will continue His work in the days ahead, completely renewing every aspect of your life.

The Bible says, "Therefore, if anyone is in Christ, he is a new creation: the old has gone, the new has come!" (2 Corinthians 5:17).

Something miraculous takes place when seed, soil, moisture, and sunlight come together. Life springs forth where there was no sign of it before. The changes that are taking place in your life are just as miraculous. This life is not something you could have generated on your own. It is yours because of God's grace.

With the advantage of hindsight, can you think of times before you were a Christian when God's grace was working through people or events in your life?

According to the Bible verse from Ephesians quoted on the previous page, what role do grace and faith play in your salvation?

According to the same verse, why is it impossible for anyone to brag about his or her own salvation?

God's *Seed* has Taken Root *In You*

God planted the seed of faith in you, and it's because of Him that you have a new life. Yet you have something to do with the process. What God does in our lives depends on the kind of soil that we provide.

Like the hard-packed soil along a footpath, some people are hardened against God. They ignore the quiet voice of God inside them that would steer them away from sinful behavior. When there are opportunities to respond to God's grace, they turn away and the seed of new life is not allowed to take root. Other influences and interests steal it away.

Perhaps there was a time when the soil of your life was hard. If so, you now have a lot to be thankful for. The grace of God has softened your heart. You have offered your life as a place where God can start something new. He has created a new life in you through His Holy Spirit. "For you have been born again, not of perishable seed, but of imperishable, through the living and enduring word of God" (1 Peter 1:23).

The seed of God's new life has been planted in you!

What can you do to keep the seed of faith growing in your heart?

Do you know some people whose hearts are hard toward God? Who?

Pray for the people you listed above, asking that God's grace would be at work in their lives.

Some people start strong in the faith but don't last long. Their hearts are like shallow ground where a plant springs up quickly but withers just as quickly in the heat. They become spiritual casualties because their initial enthusiasm for God is based only on emotion. It lacks the depth that comes from a sincere commitment of the will. Your new spiritual life needs deep roots in order to thrive.

The life of God in you may bring a flood of positive emotions. Enjoy them. Celebrate them. They are benefits of being forgiven and made clean.

Plants that Thrive
Need *Deep Roots*

But the work of God in you is not based on emotion alone. There will be times when you won't feel as happy as you do now. You must remember that God works through your faith, not through your feelings.

Faith is *belief*—belief in the plan of God. Through faith you accept the truth about yourself and about God's plan for your salvation.

Faith is also *trust*—trust in the person of Christ. Through faith you trust Him to forgive you and keep you going in this new life.

And faith is *commitment*—commitment to the purpose of God. Through faith you commit yourself to become what God wants you to be.

Emotions may change, but God's life in you is maintained by faith—by believing, trusting, and remaining committed to Him.

What is the difference between faith and feelings?

What are some of the good feelings that you have about your new life?

Why is it important to put faith into action—that is, to believe in, trust, and commit yourself to God?

The *Holy Spirit* Helps You *Grow*

J ust as weeds can choke the life from a new plant, so there are things in your life that may compete with the new life that God has created in you. You may be tempted to go back to your old way of living or feel drawn toward thoughts and actions that are not pleasing to God.

God promises, though, that these spiritual weeds need not overwhelm you. The Bible says, "No temptation has seized you except what is common to man. And God is faithful: He will not let you be tempted beyond what you can bear. But when you are tempted, He will also provide a way out so that you can stand up under it" (1 Corinthians 10:13).

The Spirit of God will help you recognize negative influences when you meet them. You have the responsibility to respond immediately and avoid them. Your spiritual growth and health depend upon your willingness to respond to God's leading.

You need God's help to keep growing. And He gives you that help through His Spirit. The Bible says, "We know that we live in Him and He in us, because He has given us of His Spirit" (1 John 4:13). Ask for God's help in prayer. Be aware of the leading of His Holy Spirit. And respond by saying "no" to those things that would smother the new life within you.

Different Christians may be tempted by different things. What are the "weeds" that are likely to trouble you, competing with God for your attention?

Pray and ask the Holy Spirit for guidance about how to rid your life of these particular weeds.

In what ways can you sense the Holy Spirit at work in your life already?

God Wants You to *Grow Strong* and *Healthy*

G od wants you to grow, and He has provided some tools that will help you do just that. These are things you can do to cultivate the new life that has started in you.

One of them is to read the Bible. It is our manual for living. Make a habit of reading it every day. If you don't know where to start, begin reading the book of John. Be open to hear what God wants to tell you about Jesus and about your new life with Him. You will be amazed at how alive this book becomes. As the Apostle Paul said, "All Scripture is God-breathed and is useful for teaching, rebuking, correcting and training in righteousness, so that the man of God may be thoroughly equipped for every good work" (2 Timothy 3:16–17).

Prayer is another gardener's tool for spiritual growth. God has given you the privilege of entering into His presence to talk things over with Him. Because you are His child, He wants you to ask Him for help when you are in need. When you pray, also listen for His quiet voice speaking to you. He wants to have a relationship with you.

Going to church is also important for your spiritual growth. God has given you a new family. Because you are a new person now, you'll be drawn to share your life with others who are part of God's family. Begin attending church each week. You will become strong and healthy as you worship, learn, and serve God with others.

Which of these "gardener's tools" are you already using?

In what ways will you benefit from Bible reading, prayer, and participating in a local church?

What can you do to ensure that each of these disciplines becomes a regular part of your life?

Bearing Fruit is in Your Future

J esus said, "If a man remains in me and I in him, he will bear much fruit.... This is to my Father's glory, that you bear much fruit, showing yourselves to be my disciples" (John 15:5, 8).

God planted His seed in you expecting a harvest. *Fruit* in a Christian's life means *character*. The Bible says, "The fruit of the Spirit is love, joy, peace, patience, kindness, goodness, faithfulness, gentleness and self-control" (Galatians 5:22–23). The seed that has been planted in you will grow into new attitudes, desires, and behaviors. As you grow, these qualities will be seen in you more and more. Their presence will demonstrate that God's Spirit is in you.

Another way that God wants you to bear fruit is by inviting others to share the new life that you've found. The changes in your life will show others that something is different about you. To that, you will want to add your spoken word about what God has done. Sharing your story with others may be just the encouragement they need to accept Christ. It will also help you grow.

Which fruits of the Spirit (from Galatians 5:22–23) are already visible in you?

Which ones are developing in your life?

Have you told anyone about your decision to follow Jesus? Name two or three people with whom you can share this good news.

RUIT

GROWING

You Can Be *Sure* That *God* Is at Work in *You*

Because God loves you, He offered new life to you. You accepted that offer when you confessed your sin, believed in Christ as your Savior, received the gift of forgiveness, and determined to live for God. God's new life entered into you.

Through faith and obedience, you have started the process of growth—allowing the life of God to go deep into your being. You will continue to grow as you learn God's Word, talk to Him in prayer, and gather with other Christians to worship.

Your life will never be the same again! You will begin to see changes in your behavior and attitudes—and so will others. You are God's newest creation! How exciting it will be to see all that God wants to make of you! "For we are God's workmanship, created in Christ Jesus . . ." (Ephesians 2:10).

The Bible says, "If we confess our sins, he is faithful and just and will forgive us our sins and purify us from all unrighteousness" (1 John 1:9). Based on this Scripture, what two things has God done for you?

The Bible also says, "Therefore, if anyone is in Christ, he is a new creation: the old has gone, the new has come!" (2 Corinthians 5:17-18). Based on these verses, what has happened to you since you believed in Christ?

MY ASSURANCE OF SALVATION

Based on the authority of God's Word,
I know that I have received a new life in Jesus Christ.

_____   _____

Your Signature   *Today's Date*

It's important that you cultivate your new life immediately. Here's a checklist of simple things you can do to put your new faith into action.

TELL SOMEONE

Find a trusted friend and tell him or her about your decision to accept Christ. This will both strengthen your faith and encourage your friend.

BEGIN READING THE BIBLE

If you don't have a Bible, ask your pastor or a Christian friend to help you purchase a version that you can easily read and understand. Begin a daily pattern of reading the Bible.

BEGIN TO PRAY

Prayer is conversation with God. Talk to Him as you would to a friend. Thank Him for what He is doing in your life. Ask Him to help

First Steps
to Help You Grow

you in areas of your life where you are struggling. Seek His direction for decisions you are making. Then spend some time quietly allowing Him to communicate with you.

GO TO CHURCH

Find a church that preaches and teaches the Bible and where you feel welcomed into its life and fellowship. You'll benefit from worshiping God with other believers.

Choose one of the following Bible verses and commit it to memory. Keep each of them in mind to encourage you on your Christian journey.

Therefore, since we have been justified through faith, we have peace with God through our Lord Jesus Christ, through whom we have gained access by faith into this grace in which we now stand. And we rejoice in the hope of the glory of God.
—Romans 5:1–2

Trust in the LORD with all your heart and lean not on your own understanding; in all your ways acknowledge Him, and He will make your paths straight.
—Proverbs 3:5–6

Ask and it will be given to you; seek and you will find; knock and the door will be opened to you.
—Matthew 7:7

What the Bible Says About the Life Growing in You

God's Grace
But God demonstrates His own love for us in this: While we were still sinners, Christ died for us.

—Romans 5:8

Faith
For it is by grace you have been saved, through faith—and this not from yourselves, it is the gift of God—not by works, so that no one can boast.

—Ephesians 2:8–9

Forgiveness
If we confess our sins, He is faithful and just and will forgive us our sins and purify us from all unrighteousness.

—I John 1:9

Assurance
Therefore, there is now no condemnation for those who are in Christ Jesus, because through Christ Jesus the law of the Spirit of life set me free from the law of sin and death.

— Romans 8:1–2

Prayer

If you remain in me and my words remain in you, ask whatever you wish, and it will be given to you.

—John 15:7

Strength for Living

So then, just as you received Christ Jesus as Lord, continue to live in Him, rooted and built up in Him, strengthened in the faith as you were taught, and overflowing with thankfulness.

—Colossians 2:6–7

Eternal Life

For the wages of sin is death, but the gift of God is eternal life in Christ Jesus our Lord.

— Romans 6:23

A GOOD START

First Steps for Growing in Your New Life in Christ

- Understand the gift that God has given you

- Take the first steps to grow in your new life

- Find the power to become a new and different person

Dr. Ken Heer was an ordained minister with The Wesleyan Church, prior to his death in 2016. He served as a pastor, educator, and church leader for more than forty years, helping people grow in Christ.

CHRISTIAN LIVING · SPIRITUAL GROWTH · DISCIPLESHIP/NEW BELIEVER
ISBN 0-89827-253-X

wesleyan
PUBLISHING HOUSE

For other life-changing resources,
visit us at wphstore.com.

9 780898 272536

90000